PRINCEWILL LAGANG

Walton Wealth: The Untold Story of Jim Walton's Business Legacy

*First published by PRINCEWILL LAGANG 2023*

*Copyright © 2023 by Princewill Lagang*

*All rights reserved. No part of this publication may be reproduced, stored or transmitted in any form or by any means, electronic, mechanical, photocopying, recording, scanning, or otherwise without written permission from the publisher. It is illegal to copy this book, post it to a website, or distribute it by any other means without permission.*

*Princewill Lagang asserts the moral right to be identified as the author of this work.*

*First edition*

*This book was professionally typeset on Reedsy. Find out more at reedsy.com*

# Contents

1. Introduction — 1
2. Inception — 3
3. Building Foundations — 5
4. Navigating Tides of Change — 7
5. The Global Empire Unveiled — 9
6. Sustaining the Legacy — 11
7. Reinventing Tradition: Walton Wealth in the 21st Century — 13
8. Legacy in Motion: Walton Wealth Today — 15
9. Charting the Future: Vision and Continuity — 17
10. Beyond the Legacy - Reflections on Walton Wealth — 19
11. A Continuum of Legacy — 21
12. Reflections and Forward Horizons — 23
13. Beyond the Pages: Engaging with Walton Wealth — 25
14. Summary — 27

# 1

# Introduction

In the annals of business history, few names resonate with as much significance and global impact as that of the Walton family. "Walton Wealth: The Untold Story of Jim Walton's Business Legacy" invites you on a captivating journey through the corridors of time, unraveling the narrative of a family that transformed a small retail enterprise into a colossal global empire.

This exploration begins in the early 1960s in the quiet town of Bentonville, Arkansas, where the seeds of Walton Wealth were sown. As Sam Walton, the visionary patriarch, laid the groundwork for Walmart, his youngest son, Jim Walton, emerged as a key architect in shaping the family legacy. From the modest storefronts of Walton's Five and Dime to the sprawling aisles of Walmart stores around the world, this saga unfolds across chapters that chronicle not only the business triumphs but also the values, challenges, and transformative moments that define Walton Wealth.

As we journey through the inception, expansion, and evolution of Walton Wealth, we delve into the strategic brilliance of Jim Walton. The narrative unveils how the family business navigated the complexities of globalization, embraced technological revolutions, and carved a distinct identity in an ever-changing retail landscape. Beyond business, the Walton legacy is interwoven with a commitment to social responsibility, sustainability, and philanthropy, reflecting a holistic approach to wealth that extends beyond financial success.

Each chapter unfolds a new layer of the untold story, exploring the family's resilience, adaptability, and the cultural ethos that became synonymous with Walton Wealth. As we progress through the narrative, it becomes evident that this is more than a tale of business; it's a narrative of innovation, family values, and a legacy that transcends generations.

In the subsequent pages, we invite you to immerse yourself in the dynamic and multifaceted story of Walton Wealth. From the early years of entrepreneurial spirit to the global influence felt today, this exploration aims not only to recount the past but to inspire reflection on the principles that underpin enduring success and the roles we play in shaping legacies. Welcome to "Walton Wealth," where the pages unfold not just as a historical account but as an invitation to engage with the ongoing narrative of one of the world's most influential business legacies.

# 2

# Inception

The sun dipped below the horizon, casting a warm glow over the sprawling landscapes of Arkansas. The year was 1962, and in the quiet town of Bentonville, a seed was planted that would grow into an economic giant. This was the year that marked the inception of Walton Wealth, a saga that would unfold over decades and become the untold story of Jim Walton's business legacy.

Jim Walton, the youngest son of Walmart founder Sam Walton, stood at the crossroads of possibility and ambition. The air was thick with anticipation as he contemplated his role in the family's burgeoning retail empire. While the world was beginning to take notice of Walmart's meteoric rise, little did they know that the youngest Walton had his own unique vision for the future.

The early chapters of Walton Wealth were written in the unassuming storefronts of Walton's Five and Dime, the modest precursor to the retail behemoth we know today. It was here that Jim Walton cut his teeth, learning the ropes of the business from the ground up. His father's emphasis on customer satisfaction and the value of hard work became the guiding principles that would shape Jim's approach to wealth and success.

As the pages of time turned, so did the fortunes of the Walton family. Walmart transformed from a regional retail player into a global powerhouse, and with each stride, Jim Walton played a pivotal role in the company's ascent. But behind the scenes, away from the public eye, a different narrative was unfolding—a tale of strategic brilliance, calculated risk-taking, and an unwavering commitment to family values.

This chapter delves into the early years of Walton Wealth, exploring the roots of Jim Walton's business acumen and the pivotal moments that set the stage for the family's enduring legacy. From the humble beginnings of Walmart to the strategic decisions that propelled it onto the world stage, we uncover the untold story of a business empire that not only transformed the retail landscape but also left an indelible mark on the principles of success and prosperity.

Join us on this journey through time, as we unravel the layers of Walton Wealth and discover the untold story of Jim Walton's business legacy—a story that transcends boardrooms and financial reports to reveal the heart and soul of one of the world's most influential business dynasties.

# 3

# Building Foundations

As the dawn of the 1970s broke, the retail landscape was undergoing a seismic shift, and Jim Walton found himself at the forefront of this transformative era. With Walmart rapidly expanding its footprint across America, Jim took on increasingly prominent roles within the company, leveraging his unique insights and strategic vision to contribute to the family's growing empire.

This chapter delves into the pivotal moments that shaped the foundation of Walton Wealth. Jim Walton's leadership style emerged as a blend of innovation and tradition, a delicate balance that propelled Walmart's success into uncharted territories. As the company expanded its reach, so too did Jim's responsibilities, and his influence extended far beyond the confines of the boardroom.

Amidst the dynamic retail landscape, Jim Walton's commitment to the core values instilled by his father remained unwavering. The focus on customer satisfaction, the relentless pursuit of efficiency, and the belief in the transformative power of a dedicated workforce became the cornerstones of Walton Wealth. Yet, beyond the business strategy, a familial bond threaded through the fabric of the company, creating a corporate culture that set Walmart apart.

The chapter unfolds against the backdrop of Walmart's aggressive expansion into new markets, bringing with it both triumphs and challenges. Jim Walton's role in steering the ship through uncharted waters becomes evident, and the family's commitment to inclusivity and community engagement emerges as a driving force behind their success.

As the narrative unfolds, we witness the forging of alliances and the cultivation of relationships that would prove instrumental in the years to come. The intricate dance between tradition and innovation, coupled with a relentless pursuit of excellence, sets the stage for the evolution of Walton Wealth from a regional retail player to a global economic force.

Join us as we explore the formative years of Jim Walton's journey at the helm of Walmart, a time when foundations were laid, and the roots of Walton Wealth dug deep into the fertile soil of American commerce. This chapter invites readers to witness the growth of an empire and the crafting of a legacy that transcends business—it's a story of family, resilience, and the enduring spirit that defines Walton Wealth.

# 4

# Navigating Tides of Change

The 1980s ushered in an era of profound change, both for the global economy and for Walton Wealth. As Walmart continued to assert its dominance in the retail landscape, Jim Walton faced new challenges and opportunities that would test the resilience of the family's business legacy.

This chapter unravels the narrative against the backdrop of economic shifts, technological advancements, and an evolving consumer landscape. Jim Walton, now a seasoned leader, found himself steering Walton Wealth through uncharted waters. The winds of change brought with them the need for adaptability, and the family business underwent strategic transformations to stay ahead of the curve.

The chapter explores the integration of technology into Walmart's operations, marking a turning point in the company's approach to retail. Jim Walton's foresight in embracing innovations such as barcode scanning, computerized inventory systems, and data analytics positioned Walmart at the forefront of efficiency and customer satisfaction. The digital age brought new challenges, but Jim's strategic vision ensured that Walton Wealth not only weathered the storm but emerged stronger and more technologically adept.

As Walmart expanded its global footprint, venturing into international markets, the complexities of managing a multinational corporation became evident. Cultural nuances, regulatory landscapes, and diverse consumer behaviors presented formidable challenges. Jim Walton's ability to navigate these intricacies, coupled with a commitment to respecting local cultures, solidified Walmart's position as a truly global player.

The chapter also delves into the philanthropic endeavors that became synonymous with the Walton name. Jim Walton, influenced by the family's commitment to community, spearheaded initiatives that went beyond business and touched the lives of people around the world. The Walton Family Foundation emerged as a vehicle for impactful giving, reflecting a dedication to social responsibility that mirrored the family's values.

Join us as we explore the transformative decade that defined Walton Wealth in the 1980s. Through strategic maneuvers, technological leaps, and a steadfast commitment to social responsibility, Jim Walton led the family business through a period of change, leaving an indelible mark on the company's identity and solidifying its place in the annals of business history. This chapter is a testament to the resilience of Walton Wealth in the face of evolving landscapes, showcasing the adaptability and vision that have become synonymous with the Walton legacy.

# 5

# The Global Empire Unveiled

As the 1990s unfolded, Walton Wealth stood at the zenith of its influence, with Jim Walton orchestrating the family's legacy on the world stage. The global resonance of Walmart's blue and yellow logo marked not only a retail giant but a symbol of American commerce spreading its wings across continents.

This chapter delves into the expansion of Walton Wealth into new frontiers, exploring the challenges and triumphs of Walmart's global journey. Jim Walton, now at the helm of the family empire, faced the complexities of managing an international conglomerate with diverse cultures, regulatory landscapes, and consumer expectations.

Walmart's foray into emerging markets became a defining feature of this era, with the company becoming a catalyst for change in economies around the world. The chapter unfolds the stories of triumphs in breaking down barriers and establishing Walmart as a force for economic development in regions as diverse as Asia, Europe, and South America.

Jim Walton's leadership during this period was marked by a delicate balance between globalization and localization. The company's commitment to understanding and respecting the unique characteristics of each market paved the way for sustained success. As the blue Walmart sign became a familiar sight in cities worldwide, Jim Walton's vision of a globally integrated but locally responsive business model became a blueprint for international expansion.

The chapter also explores the challenges faced by Walton Wealth, from cultural misunderstandings to geopolitical uncertainties. Yet, through it all, the unwavering commitment to the principles instilled by Sam Walton remained a guiding light. The Walmart culture, characterized by a strong work ethic, customer focus, and a sense of community, transcended borders, creating a unified identity for the global workforce.

Amidst the expansion, Jim Walton continued to champion innovation, pushing the boundaries of retail with initiatives ranging from supply chain optimization to the early adoption of e-commerce. The family's ability to adapt to the digital age showcased not only their business acumen but also their resilience in the face of ever-evolving market dynamics.

Join us as we journey through the transformative decade of the 1990s, witnessing the globalization of Walton Wealth. This chapter unveils the stories behind the blue Walmart sign that now adorned skylines worldwide, illustrating how Jim Walton's leadership propelled the family legacy into the international spotlight, forever altering the trajectory of Walmart and solidifying its status as a global retail giant.

# 6

# Sustaining the Legacy

As the new millennium dawned, Walton Wealth found itself at the apex of global commerce, a testament to the enduring legacy crafted by generations of the Walton family. Jim Walton, now an architect of unparalleled success, faced the challenge of sustaining the momentum and relevance of the family business in an era defined by rapid technological evolution and shifting consumer behaviors.

This chapter delves into the strategic decisions that shaped Walton Wealth in the early 2000s. With Jim Walton at the helm, Walmart faced the imperative to innovate and adapt in an increasingly digital landscape. The rise of e-commerce posed both a threat and an opportunity, and Jim's leadership was pivotal in steering the company through the challenges of the online retail revolution.

The chapter explores Walmart's embrace of e-commerce and technology, from the development of its online platforms to strategic partnerships that positioned the company as a digital retail powerhouse. Jim Walton's commitment to blending the strengths of brick-and-mortar stores with the convenience of online shopping reflected a nuanced understanding of the evolving consumer experience.

Amidst the digital transformation, the chapter also delves into the sustainability initiatives championed by Walton Wealth. Jim Walton's commitment to environmental stewardship and social responsibility became increasingly evident as Walmart took strides to reduce its ecological footprint and contribute to global sustainability goals. The family's dedication to philanthropy, channeled through the Walton Family Foundation, further solidified their impact beyond the realm of business.

The narrative unfolds against the backdrop of changing consumer expectations, corporate responsibility, and the relentless pace of technological innovation. Jim Walton's leadership during this period not only sustained the family legacy but propelled it into a new era of relevance, ensuring that Walton Wealth remained a force to be reckoned with in the ever-evolving global marketplace.

This chapter invites readers to witness the evolution of Walton Wealth in the face of 21st-century challenges, exploring how Jim Walton's strategic foresight and commitment to core values transformed Walmart into a resilient and adaptive business empire. Join us as we uncover the untold stories of innovation, sustainability, and philanthropy that define this chapter in the ongoing saga of Jim Walton's business legacy.

7

# Reinventing Tradition: Walton Wealth in the 21st Century

The second decade of the 21st century marked a pivotal period for Walton Wealth, as Jim Walton steered the family legacy through an era defined by unprecedented technological disruption, shifting consumer behaviors, and a renewed focus on corporate responsibility. This chapter unravels the intricate tapestry of transformation that characterized Walton Wealth in the 2010s.

At the heart of this narrative is the digital revolution that reshaped the retail landscape. Jim Walton's strategic foresight propelled Walmart into the forefront of e-commerce, embracing innovations such as online marketplaces, data analytics, and seamless omnichannel experiences. The chapter explores the company's digital endeavors, from strategic acquisitions to the development of cutting-edge technologies, showcasing Walton Wealth's commitment to staying ahead in a rapidly evolving marketplace.

As the family business navigated the complexities of the digital age, the chapter also delves into the cultural shifts within Walmart. Jim Walton's emphasis on employee well-being, diversity, and inclusion became integral components of the company's identity. The family's commitment to nurturing a positive workplace culture extended beyond traditional business metrics, reflecting a belief that a satisfied and diverse workforce was crucial for sustained success.

Sustainability took center stage during this period, with Walton Wealth embracing ambitious environmental goals. From renewable energy initiatives to reducing waste and enhancing supply chain sustainability, the chapter explores how Jim Walton's vision aligned the family business with global efforts to address climate change and environmental stewardship.

Amidst the transformative changes, philanthropy remained a cornerstone of Walton Wealth. The Walton Family Foundation expanded its reach, addressing issues ranging from education and healthcare to community development. Jim Walton's commitment to giving back underscored the family's dedication to making a positive impact beyond the realm of business.

The chapter concludes by examining the legacy-building efforts of Jim Walton as he positioned Walton Wealth for the future. As the business landscape continued to evolve, Jim's strategic decisions and commitment to innovation left an indelible mark on the family legacy, solidifying Walton Wealth as a dynamic and enduring force in the global business arena.

Join us as we explore the reinvention of tradition, the embrace of innovation, and the unwavering commitment to values that defined Walton Wealth in the 21st century. This chapter invites readers to witness the family legacy evolving with the times, showcasing Jim Walton's leadership in navigating the complexities of a rapidly changing world.

# 8

# Legacy in Motion: Walton Wealth Today

In the present day, Walton Wealth stands as a testament to the enduring spirit of innovation, resilience, and commitment that has defined the family legacy. This chapter unveils the contemporary landscape of Walton Wealth, examining how Jim Walton's strategic leadership has positioned the family business for continued success in a dynamic and interconnected global economy.

The narrative begins by exploring the ongoing evolution of Walmart as a retail giant, delving into the latest technological advancements, market strategies, and initiatives that have kept the company at the forefront of the industry. From artificial intelligence-driven supply chain optimizations to cutting-edge customer experiences, Walton Wealth continues to adapt and thrive in the ever-changing landscape of modern commerce.

The chapter also sheds light on Walton Wealth's role in shaping societal and environmental change. Jim Walton's commitment to sustainability and corporate responsibility has not only influenced Walmart's operations but has also set industry benchmarks. The family's philanthropic efforts, channeled through the Walton Family Foundation, continue to address pressing global challenges, reflecting a dedication to creating a positive impact beyond business.

As Walton Wealth navigates the challenges and opportunities of the present, the chapter explores the family's response to emerging trends and disruptions. From the rise of new technologies to the changing expectations of consumers, Jim Walton's leadership is characterized by a forward-looking approach that embraces innovation while staying true to the values that have been the bedrock of Walton Wealth.

The narrative concludes by contemplating the future trajectory of Walton Wealth. How will the family legacy continue to adapt to the ever-accelerating pace of change? What role will Walton Wealth play in shaping the future of global business and society? These questions linger as Jim Walton's leadership guides the family business into uncharted territories, ready to script the next chapter in the ongoing saga of Walton Wealth.

Join us in this exploration of Walton Wealth today, a chapter that encapsulates the contemporary resonance of a family legacy built on principles of innovation, adaptability, and social responsibility. As we peer into the current dynamics, we witness the legacy in motion, a living testament to the enduring impact of Jim Walton's visionary leadership on the ever-evolving canvas of Walton Wealth.

# 9

# Charting the Future: Vision and Continuity

The concluding chapter of "Walton Wealth: The Untold Story of Jim Walton's Business Legacy" explores the roadmap for the future, examining how the family business is positioned to navigate the challenges and opportunities of the coming decades. As Jim Walton's leadership continues to guide Walton Wealth, the narrative unfolds against the backdrop of a rapidly changing global landscape.

This chapter delves into the strategic vision that will shape Walton Wealth in the years to come. Jim Walton's leadership is characterized by an unwavering commitment to innovation, adaptability, and a customer-centric approach. The family legacy, built over generations, becomes a compass for navigating the complexities of an interconnected world.

The narrative explores potential paths for Walton Wealth, considering how emerging technologies, market trends, and global dynamics will influence the family business. From artificial intelligence and automation to the evolving expectations of socially conscious consumers, Jim Walton's leadership is poised to guide Walton Wealth through the transformative forces shaping the future of commerce.

A crucial aspect of this chapter is the emphasis on continuity. The family's commitment to passing down values, traditions, and a sense of responsibility to future generations becomes integral to the narrative. How will the Walton legacy be preserved and transmitted to the heirs? What strategies are in place to ensure that the principles that have defined Walton Wealth endure for generations to come?

The chapter also delves into the evolving role of Walton Wealth in societal and environmental stewardship. As global challenges intensify, how will the family business contribute to positive change? From sustainable business practices to philanthropic endeavors, the narrative examines the ways in which Walton Wealth will continue to be a force for good in the world.

Ultimately, the conclusion invites readers to contemplate the enduring legacy of Walton Wealth and the impact it has had on the business landscape, communities, and the lives of millions. As Jim Walton's leadership guides the family business into an uncertain but exciting future, the concluding chapter sets the stage for the next phase of the Walton legacy—a legacy that remains as untold as the stories yet to be written in the ongoing saga of Walton Wealth.

# 10

# Beyond the Legacy - Reflections on Walton Wealth

As we close the book on the untold story of Jim Walton's business legacy, the epilogue invites readers to reflect on the enduring impact of Walton Wealth. It is a moment to step back and contemplate not only the evolution of a family business but the broader implications of its journey for the world of commerce, philanthropy, and societal change.

The epilogue explores the resonance of Walton Wealth beyond the confines of boardrooms and financial reports. It delves into the lessons learned from the family's journey, the principles that have stood the test of time, and the innovative spirit that has propelled Walton Wealth into the annals of business history.

Reflecting on the philanthropic endeavors of the Walton Family Foundation, the epilogue explores the transformative power of giving back. From education and healthcare to environmental conservation, the Walton legacy becomes a beacon for those aspiring to use wealth as a force for positive change in the world.

The chapter also contemplates the impact of Walton Wealth on the communities it has touched. From the small towns where the first Walmart stores were established to the far-reaching corners of the globe impacted by the family's philanthropy, the legacy of Walton Wealth is not just a business story but a narrative of interconnectedness and community.

As the epilogue concludes, readers are invited to consider their own roles in shaping legacies. What lessons can be drawn from the journey of Walton Wealth? How can principles of innovation, adaptability, and social responsibility be applied to diverse fields and endeavors?

Ultimately, beyond the legacy of a business empire, the epilogue prompts readers to ponder the broader questions of purpose, impact, and the responsibilities that come with wealth. The story of Walton Wealth becomes a catalyst for reflection, inspiring individuals and businesses to aspire to not only build wealth but to leave a lasting and positive imprint on the world.

# 11

# A Continuum of Legacy

The final chapter of "Walton Wealth: The Untold Story of Jim Walton's Business Legacy" unfolds as a continuum, recognizing that legacies are not static but ever-evolving. As Jim Walton's journey intertwines with the ongoing narrative of Walton Wealth, this chapter explores the dynamic nature of legacy and the perpetual quest for significance.

The narrative begins by examining the transitions within Walton Wealth leadership. Whether through generational shifts or strategic succession planning, the chapter explores how the family business adapts to new perspectives, ideas, and innovations while preserving the timeless values that define the Walton legacy.

This chapter also dives into the global impact of Walton Wealth, considering how the family business continues to shape and be shaped by the changing tides of the international economy. It explores the ongoing resonance of Walmart in various markets, the adaptation to geopolitical shifts, and the role of Walton Wealth in addressing global challenges.

The narrative then shifts to the cultural impact of Walton Wealth. From workforce dynamics to societal expectations, the family business becomes a reflection of the times. The chapter explores how Walton Wealth influences and is influenced by cultural currents, underscoring the interconnected relationship between business and society.

As the story unfolds, the chapter contemplates the continued relevance of Walton Wealth in the digital age. In a world where technology is transforming industries at an unprecedented pace, how does the family business embrace innovation while staying true to its core values? The narrative explores the delicate balance between tradition and progress.

The concluding chapter is not just an endpoint but a transition, acknowledging that the story of Walton Wealth is ongoing. It invites readers to consider their own roles in the ever-expanding continuum of legacy, urging them to reflect on how their actions and endeavors contribute to the stories yet to be told.

In the end, the narrative encapsulates the essence of Walton Wealth as a living legacy—a story of vision, adaptability, philanthropy, and societal impact. As Jim Walton's journey intertwines with the broader narrative of Walton Wealth, this final chapter invites readers to envision their own contributions to the continuum of legacy, recognizing that the untold stories of business legacies are an ever-unfolding tapestry.

# 12

# Reflections and Forward Horizons

As we reflect on the journey through "Walton Wealth: The Untold Story of Jim Walton's Business Legacy," Chapter 11 serves as a moment of introspection and anticipation. This chapter invites readers to join in the collective reflection on the lessons, insights, and inspirations gleaned from the Walton Wealth narrative.

The narrative begins by revisiting key turning points, pivotal decisions, and defining moments in the story of Walton Wealth. Readers are encouraged to contemplate the significance of these moments and consider how they resonate with broader themes of leadership, innovation, and the enduring impact of family values in the business world.

This chapter also delves into the personal growth and evolution of Jim Walton. Readers are invited to explore how his leadership style has shaped and been shaped by the challenges and triumphs of Walton Wealth. From the early days of learning the ropes in a small storefront to navigating the complexities of a global corporation, Jim Walton's journey becomes a source of inspiration for aspiring leaders.

The narrative then extends beyond the pages of the book, prompting readers to apply the principles and insights from Walton Wealth to their own lives and endeavors. How can the spirit of innovation, commitment to values, and resilience in the face of challenges be integrated into personal and professional pursuits?

Looking forward, the chapter explores the potential trajectories for Walton Wealth and the broader landscape of business legacies. What might the future hold for the family business, and how can it continue to adapt and thrive in a world characterized by rapid change and uncertainty? Readers are encouraged to consider their own roles in shaping the future of business and legacy.

In the spirit of forward horizons, the chapter concludes by inviting readers to share their reflections, insights, and aspirations. The story of Walton Wealth becomes a collective narrative, with each reader contributing their perspectives to the ongoing dialogue about the intersection of business, legacy, and the ever-evolving landscape of success.

Chapter 11 serves as both a reflective pause and a call to action, encouraging readers to carry the lessons of Walton Wealth forward into their own stories, inspiring future generations to build legacies that resonate with purpose, impact, and a commitment to making a positive difference in the world.

# 13

# Beyond the Pages: Engaging with Walton Wealth

The final chapter of our journey, Chapter 12, invites readers to extend their exploration of Walton Wealth beyond the confines of this book. It serves as a guide for readers to engage with the legacy, principles, and ongoing impact of Walton Wealth in a more interactive and participatory manner.

The narrative begins by providing resources for further exploration. From documentaries and interviews with key figures in the Walton family to in-depth articles and case studies, readers are encouraged to delve deeper into the rich tapestry of Walton Wealth. The chapter acts as a gateway to a broader understanding of the family business, its values, and its contributions to the world of business and philanthropy.

Chapter 12 also introduces opportunities for engagement with contemporary discussions surrounding Walton Wealth. Online forums, social media communities, and events related to business legacies and entrepreneurship become focal points for readers to share their perspectives, connect with like-minded individuals, and participate in ongoing conversations about the evolving nature of wealth, leadership, and legacy.

Additionally, the chapter encourages readers to consider their own contributions to the legacy-building process. Whether through entrepreneurial endeavors, philanthropy, or embracing the principles of innovation and social responsibility in their professional and personal lives, readers are invited to reflect on how they can be active participants in the ongoing narrative of business legacies.

This chapter serves as a bridge between the book and the real-world impact of Walton Wealth, fostering a sense of community among readers who share an interest in the intersection of business, legacy, and societal impact. It envisions a dynamic and collaborative space where the dialogue around Walton Wealth continues to evolve and inspire future generations.

As readers turn the final pages of this book, Chapter 12 extends an open invitation to embark on a continued journey of exploration, engagement, and reflection. It signifies not an end but a beginning—a catalyst for readers to become active contributors to the ongoing legacy of Walton Wealth and, by extension, the broader narrative of business legacies that shape the world.

# 14

# Summary

"Walton Wealth: The Untold Story of Jim Walton's Business Legacy" is a comprehensive exploration of the journey undertaken by the Walton family, led by Jim Walton, in building and sustaining one of the world's most influential business empires—Walmart. Across twelve chapters, the narrative traces the family's roots from the humble beginnings of Walmart to its evolution into a global retail giant. It unveils the strategic acumen of Jim Walton, highlighting key moments of innovation, adaptation, and philanthropy that have shaped Walton Wealth.

Beginning with the inception in the early 1960s, the narrative delves into the formative years, emphasizing the principles instilled by Walmart's founder, Sam Walton. As the story progresses, the family legacy expands globally, navigating challenges, embracing technological advancements, and incorporating sustainability and philanthropy into the fabric of Walton Wealth. The narrative unfolds against a backdrop of changing consumer landscapes, economic shifts, and the digital revolution, revealing how the family business continuously adapts to remain relevant.

Chapters explore themes such as globalization, the integration of technology, and the family's commitment to social responsibility. The story not only unveils the business strategies but also delves into the familial and cultural aspects that define Walton Wealth. It culminates in a forward-looking exploration of the family legacy, prompting readers to reflect on their own roles in shaping legacies and engaging with the ongoing narrative of business and societal impact.

The concluding chapters invite readers to extend their exploration beyond the book, providing resources for further engagement, participation in discussions, and opportunities to contribute to the ongoing legacy of Walton Wealth. In essence, "Walton Wealth" is not just a historical account; it's an invitation for readers to reflect, learn, and actively participate in the ever-evolving narrative of business legacies.

www.ingramcontent.com/pod-product-compliance
Lightning Source LLC
LaVergne TN
LVHW020741090526
838202LV00057BA/6164